W9-BFL-347

About the Getting to Know *Series*

This round-the-world series not only covers everyday life in many countries and regions and includes their geography and history — it also highlights *what's new today.* The series offers timely — and often first — reports on the birth of new nations in Africa and Asia, the splitting of ancient nations like China, the let's-get-together movement of members of Europe's and Latin America's Common Markets, and the struggles of two thirds of the world to attain the good life possessed by the other third. *To keep each book up to date in these fast-changing times, it is revised with every new printing.*

Specific countries in the *Getting to Know* series are determined by a survey of curriculum specialists in the fifty states. Made every two years, the survey is used to relate GTK subject matter to classroom needs. To insure intimacy as well as immediacy, authors are chosen first of all for the quality of their personal experience with the subject matter. All *Getting to Knows* are also checked by experts prior to publication.

GETTING TO KNOW THE U·S·A·

by Charles W. Ferguson

illustrated by Leonard Everett Fisher

COWARD-McCANN, Inc.   NEW YORK

DEDICATION

*To my grandsons Sean and Kevin Ferguson
with confidence that their ideas will be as big
as the land of their birth*

Author and publishers wish to acknowledge with appreciation the thoughtful reviews of this book in manuscript form and the many valuable suggestions provided by Allan Nevins, Dr. S. P. McCutchen, Chairman of the Department of Social Studies at New York University's School of Education, and Walden Moore, Director of the Declaration on Atlantic Unity and formerly Professor of Government at the University of Rochester.

08-012
Sixth Impression

Text © 1963 by Charles W. Ferguson

Illustrations © 1963 by Leonard Everett Fisher

All rights reserved. This book, or parts thereof, may not be reproduced in any form without permission in writing from the publishers. Published simultaneously in the Dominion of Canada by Longmans Canada Limited, Toronto.

Library of Congress Catalog Card Number: 63-10173

Editor of this series: Sabra Holbrook

MANUFACTURED IN THE UNITED STATES OF AMERICA

973

F

ABOUT THE BOOK

With this book, the *Getting to Know* Series celebrates its tenth anniversary—and does so by coming back home from the 51 foreign regions it has covered since 1953. The *U.S.A.* is the 52nd *GTK*.

In it, Mr. Ferguson conceives of our country as a giant. He shows how the size of the North American continent has, from the days of early explorers to the present, shaped events, people, inventions and especially spirit.

We watch the process of America becoming civilized, partly as a result of the influence of its women. We also watch the giant battle with the machine which comes to replace myth-heroes of the wilderness and we see the machine, tamed and put to use, actually perform feats of conquest attributed to the old-time folkgods.

Most of the people we meet are not famous; they are not heroes of history for this is *not a history book*. It is mainly a story of ordinary souls who became extraordinary as they dare to undertake tasks that the size of America demands.

The people we get to know are Chinese and Irish railroad workers; they are pioneer women like Mrs. Tamsen Donner, who, when caught in the snows of the Sierra Nevada mountains on a westward trek, took her three daughters to meet a rescue party and returned to die with her husband who was too weak to travel. They are hunters of buffalo and men like Walking Coyote, an Indian who sought to preserve the vanishing animals. They are Boy Scouts placing markers at the opening of the Lincoln Highway. They are inventors like George Hulett, who designed the first machine for unloading iron ore from ships. They are people who have come from many other lands bringing gifts of skill and strength: they are the Shaunneseys, Smiths, Stanislowskis, Schultzes, Sadis, Wallaces, Rosenfields and Monets—all living on the same street.

As we make their acquaintance, we discover how size has affected our language, our form of government and most important of all, our ideas. We watch our program to aid other nations grow as our own nation grows in strength. And finally, with the President of the United States, we foresee the possibility of an "Atlantic partnership . . . between the new Union emerging in Europe and the old American union founded here 175 years ago." "Whatever we do," the author promises, "we'll do it in a big way."

ABOUT THE AUTHOR

Texas-born CHARLES FERGUSON, a Senior Editor at The Reader's Digest since 1942, is also author of the best-selling study of Cardinal Wolsey and his times: *Naked to Mine Enemies*. Among his other books are: *A Little Democracy is a Dangerous Thing* and *Say It With Words*. He is also a contributor to many magazines.

A graduate of Southern Methodist University in Dallas, Mr. Ferguson served for two years as a Methodist minister in Booker and Fort Worth; for a year as Foreign Service Reserve Officer attached to the United States Embassy in London and more recently, for a year as Lecturer on Language for Laymen at the New School for Social Research in New York.

He is a member of the National Council of the Boy Scouts of America and a sought-after speaker before such diverse audiences as the National Congress of Parents and Teachers and dock-side political clubs in South Wales. He lives on Apple Tree Hill in Mount Kisco, New York.

ABOUT THE ILLUSTRATOR

A native New Yorker who now lives in Westport, LEONARD FISHER received his training from Yale University's School of Fine Art. A Pulitzer Art Prize winner, his experience includes painting a mural in Affreville, Algeria, for the U.S. Army, decorating a military hospital in Hawaii for the Red Cross, and illustrating more than 75 children's books, in connection with which he has taken part in Children's Book Week programs across the country. His paintings have appeared in many exhibitions.

AMERICA is a giant living in a castle made up of mighty mountains, with oceans and a sea for moats, with great prairies for lawns, fit for seven-league boots to stalk across. It is a giant with an appetite as big as itself and with the energy of a thunderstorm. Its buildings, its factories, its farms, its government, its hopes — everything about it is big, big, big.

It isn't biggest. We have neither as much land nor as many people as the Soviet Union or China. We don't have as much land as neighboring Canada although we have more people. Never mind. Our awareness of the great size we are has colored our thinking, crept into our speech and compelled a good many of our actions.

For instance, in the U.S.A. we tend to think of ourselves as being America itself. Any Canadian will tell you — fast and emphatically — that America means Canada as well. A child in Nova Scotia may sing "America the Beautiful" without ever thinking that the words speak of the United States. A child in Chile may call himself an Americano. To Latin Americans the term may take in the hemisphere.

It does in fact. All the land from Labrador to the Strait of Magellan was given the name America by the map maker Gerhardus Mercator in 1541. Yet we choose to apply the name to the United States.

So if you are going to understand the U.S.A., you are going to have to take the measure of it that the land we call America has always taken of itself. Once you recognize the feeling of strength that comes from our sense of size, you get an insight into matters that might otherwise remain a kettle of odd and squirming facts.

Start by standing off to see how America looks from afar. It towers. Even some of its trees — sequoia and redwood — tower. And its towers tower. The word *skyscraper* is now an everyday term, but think of it as if it were being used for the first time. Though skyscrapers were first built in crowded areas, the architecture caught on. Here was a land with endless land, yet it often chose to make its buildings scrape the heavens. It looked to the blue above as a part of its territory and developed such

6

practices as skywriting with airplanes penciling in letters of smoke ten miles high.

Prime Minister Nehru of India remarked on his first visit here in 1949 that nobody should have to see America for the first time! It is too vast to grasp or believe all at once.

A shipload of children who recently arrived in San Francisco from the Philippines might have appreciated his remark. They came for a year's study under the American Field Service program of sending young Americans abroad and inviting young people from all over the world to come and see us. The children were overwhelmed by the spectacular size of all they saw and by dinnertime they felt a need to recall something sizable in their own land. Brussels sprouts were served, and one Filipino girl noted with some pride, "The cabbages are bigger than this in the Philippines."

America makes visitors, young and old, think of size. A distinguished French sculptor, Frédéric Auguste Bartholdi, who came to see us in 1871, wrote to a friend in France, "Everything in America is big! Here, even the peas are big."

Among other great sights, Bartholdi had seen our redwoods, some of them 350 feet high and 20 feet around. His idea of a gift from the people of France to the people of the United States was a statue of Liberty Enlightening the World. After his visit, Bartholdi was convinced that the statue must be nothing short of colossal — the biggest in the world.

"I propose," he said, "to make a statue that can be seen from the shores of America to the shores of France." His proposal was exaggerated but it was in keeping with our spirit. When the Statue of Liberty was finally set on Bedloe's Island off the shores of New York in 1886 its lamp rose 305 feet from the foundation — almost as high as the redwoods.

Even before America was explored, it had a legend of size. The reports of John Cabot, who sailed on voyages of discovery under grants from King Henry VII of England in 1497 and 1498, lit

the imagination those who stayed at home. Not only was the new land endless, or so it seemed as John Cabot sailed south from northern points along the coast, but even the fish were big and the supply of them beyond belief. They could be caught in weighted baskets. Here, beyond the fish-filled waters, was a never-never land, the shore of which stretched farther than imagination could follow. What must lie behind that shore!

The fame of America and its baffling size were early advertised by words and pictures throughout Europe. Beginning in 1590 and for forty years thereafter, a Belgian named Theodore DeBry published in Frankfort, Germany, all the writings he could find about America. In all, DeBry produced 27 huge volumes, each illustrated with many engravings. The first volume was translated into four languages. Later books were in German and Latin.

This flood of news and pictures, together with the tales of traders and explorers — English, French and Spanish — excited the imagination of Europeans and made the venturesome want to come and see for themselves.

Stunned by the reported size of the land mass called America, cautious Englishmen, used to islands at home, made their earliest settlements on islands here. Under the direction of Sir Walter Raleigh, the first English colonists settled on Roanoke Island, off the coast of what is now North Carolina. Two years later the settlers had vanished — nor was any trace of them ever found. It was as if they had been swallowed. The second group, coming from England in 1607, made their homes on Jamestown Island in a sheltered river of Virginia.

The island was a peninsula when the tide was out and gradually these English nosed inland. The inland seemed to have no end to it. When the settlers reached the mountains to the west, it was as if the mountains were guardians of some mysterious, wooded kingdom. These mountains were twice as high (and must have looked ten times as high) as the Cheviot Hills and the Pennines back home in England. Here surely

was a home for giants. Only giants could possess such country and put it to use.

Farther on were enormous inland seas later called Great Lakes. The Ohio River, which led west, was five times as long as the Thames in England and twice as long as the Seine in France. And the Ohio emptied its great wash into the Mississippi, which the Indians called the Father of Waters, and the Mississippi was ten times as long as the Thames and at points it was so wide that it looked as broad as the Straits of Dover separating England from France.

Even the simple facts were stupendous and you can imagine how they fed the fancy when they were carried back to tiny England or to rural France or to a Spain hemmed in by mountains and habits of living unchanged for generations.

Gradually, as the vision of America grew, it seemed infinite. A king, with a flick of his wrist, would grant to a favorite or to some enterprising fellow a territory greater than all that the monarch ruled at home. In 1681 William Penn secured in payment of a debt rights that almost equaled the 50,327 square miles that made up England. Oglethorpe and nineteen associates received from King George II lands even bigger than England and three times larger than Holland.

Visitors noticed that the size of the land had a very real effect on the thinking and habits of those who lived in it. Even in early days tourists came to see the sights and judge whether they were as advertised. These observers saw and wrote about things that people who had settled here and were wresting a living from the soil and waters were too busy to see.

One effect visitors noticed was the desire to move about. There was a touch of the explorer in most Americans. They didn't like to stay put. If they didn't hike out to settle inland, they rode out in big wagons or on horseback to see the rest of the country or to trade in markets. In 1818, an English visitor named Morris Birkbeck noted that the people of America "are great travelers and in general better acquainted with the vast expanse of the country than the English with their little island."

Distance and the impulse to cover it put giddyap into everything we did. In one year 12,000 great wagons, each drawn by four to six horses, passed between Baltimore and Philadelphia; and in that same year the road between Philadelphia and Pittsburgh, crossed by five mountain ranges, became a thoroughfare lined with wagons. Mr. Birkbeck from England, goggle-eyed, wrote: "Add to these . . . innumerable travelers on horseback, on foot, and in light wagons, and you have before you a scene of bustle and business, extending over a space of 300 miles, which is truly wonderful."

Size and distance influenced the conveyances we built. Most famous of all was the Conestoga wagon, named for the town in Lancaster County, Pennsylvania, where it was made. The Conestoga had remarkable features. Its body was shaped like a canoe and the shape prevented goods from sliding around when the wagon traveled over mountain roads. But chiefly it had size. It had big, sturdy wheels, with iron tires six inches wide, to support heavy loads. Six to eight horses were needed to pull it. When fully loaded, the Conestoga could carry 12,000 pounds — as much as a small truck today.

Distance was something we had come to count on — and with good reason. It had been one of our allies in the war in which we won our freedom from British rule, the war of the American Revolution. Not only did Great Britain have to transport troops across thousands of miles of open sea before she could attack at all, but after the troops arrived they had to be maneuvered over immense areas of unfriendly land. At least twice during the war, distance helped the Americans and frustrated the British in decisive fashion.

The first time was in 1777 when British General Sir John Burgoyne moved down from Canada with heavy arms and a huge baggage train, hoping to take control of the Hudson River and separate New England from the other colonies. At first his march was a triumph. Fort Ticonderoga in upper New York fell to him.

Two months later, however, Burgoyne's supplies were gone and it was too far to go back to Canada for more. He sent troops east to seize American supplies at Bennington, Vermont, but the attempt failed miserably. After wallowing around and fighting forests and distances as well as Americans, Burgoyne finally surrendered near Saratoga, New York.

The second crisis created by distance began in 1780. General Sir Henry Clinton took his army down from New York by sea and captured Charleston, South Carolina. Then Clinton returned to New York, leaving British armies in the far South under the command of Lord Cornwallis, who pushed his way into Virginia.

There followed a high-flown dispute between the two generals over the strategy to be followed next. They argued back and forth by post, with each letter taking a week or ten days to reach its destination — while in the meantime guerrilla bands of frontiersmen and Indians from the Appalachian Mountains struck swiftly at Cornwallis' army, harassing it at every turn.

Finally Clinton cut the argument off by ordering Cornwallis to take a position on Yorktown Peninsula. General George Washington learned of the order. Knowing he could count on the French fleet to aid him in nearby waters, he moved his army to Virginia. Trapped by American and French forces, Cornwallis surrendered on October 19, 1781. That very same day Clinton, not knowing what was going on way down in Virginia, set out from New York with 7,000 useless reinforcements.

But when the war was over and peace with Great Britain was signed in 1783, the distances that had helped win the war began to threaten the unity of the winners. There was the danger that settlers in the West, along the Mississippi, might feel closer to the people of New Orleans, then under the control of Spain, or to the British in Canada, than to the Americans of the thirteen states.

The movement west had begun in earnest thirteen years before the outbreak of the Revolution and the war had not stopped it. Washington understood that something must be done to keep the two sections

of the new America together. Hardly had he taken his farewell of his officers and put in for a brief rest at his home in Mount Vernon when he set off on a trip to the western country he had known as a young surveyor and soldier. There he found problems even more serious than he had imagined. "The western settlers," he declared, "stand as it were upon a pivot. The touch of a feather would turn them any way."

During the Revolution the country had been in effect thirteen separate countries. They called themselves states and they had joined in a Confederation, which was a loose alliance, to fight the British. But each state had kept its own frontier. These frontiers made America into an imitation of Europe. A lot of small countries, each proud of its own rights, didn't suit the circumstances of the new and vast land.

To revise the Confederation, 55 men from twelve of the states (all but Rhode Island) came together in May 1787. Missing were some who had been active in the events that led to the Revolution. Thomas Jefferson, who had drafted the Declaration of Independence eleven years before, was in France. John Adams, who had been on the committee to help him, was in England. His cousin, Samuel Adams, who had led the fireworks against British rule in New England, was opposed to a stronger government. So was that ardent patriot and orator, Patrick Henry. Both stayed away.

But younger men came to Philadelphia, notably James Madison, thirty-six, who was to become the fourth President of the United States, and Alexander Hamilton, thirty, who was to become Washington's Secretary of the Treasury. They were already eager to grapple with the new problems of the new world. This young generation was joined by such wise old heads as Benjamin Franklin and by Robert Morris, the man whose skill had helped finance the Revolution. And Washington presided over the proceedings and gave them dignity by his presence.

Dignity was needed. The talk went on for a hundred days — all during the summer and into September — and often it was bitter. Each state wanted to make sure of its own particular rights, each state had an issue — and the issue of slavery was one of the sharpest. Five of the Northern states — Massachusetts, New Hampshire, Pennsylvania, Connecticut and Rhode Island — had decided against slavery. If these states could decide against it, Southern states felt, they should be allowed to decide for it. And in the end so they were, although a twenty-year limit was placed on their right to import slaves.

It was further agreed that three out of every five slaves should be counted in determining the population of the Southern states, an important decision for the South because the number of representatives in the lower house of the new government was to be based on population.

Out of all the argument and compromise came an inspired idea. The idea was a federal system of government, a system providing for each state to look after its own affairs with such laws as it needed, but with the defense of all the states and other matters affecting the welfare of all delegated to a central government. The central government was given the power to coin money, to take charge of the mails, to regulate interstate and international trade and conduct foreign affairs, to maintain an army and navy, to tax citizens directly. It could make laws to be observed in all the states — and it could enforce them. Certain rights were taken from the states, among them the right to form alliances and to impose taxes on goods from other states.

In the past, cities and countries had banded together in leagues for trade or defense, but each had carefully kept the right to do as it pleased in a showdown. Never before had there been such a strong federal system. The Constitution that defined it was not only new in this country, it was new in political history.

Yet, while providing for national security, the new government also provided for local freedom. The states were left free to make laws against crimes of violence, to determine which citizens could vote, and to act upon many matters that didn't affect the welfare of the whole nation.

The states did not accept this Constitution immediately. They debated it for two years in the press and on the platform, but at last it was

adopted by all except North Carolina and tiny Rhode Island, which soon joined the union formed by the rest. By 1789 the U.S.A. was officially in business. The local citizen was also a citizen of the whole. The lines drawn by state boundaries were no longer frontiers.

The only frontier was a common national one and there were plenty of men and women ready out of habit to move across it. The young country was now ready to expand and get as big as all outdoors.

Wherever enough people settled, they could form another state. The old Confederation had made such a rule and the new federal government continued it. And so the giant began to stride with tremendous paces across the vast continent toward the Pacific. Within sixty years it had bought from France a territory much bigger than France and, after this purchase of Louisiana, it had gobbled up New Mexico, Arizona, Texas and California from Mexico, considered taking over Cuba, and had opened great veins of gold near San Francisco.

To possess and settle the wilderness and move out into the great empty spaces called for men larger than life. And that is how the men who took leading parts in the venture came to be pictured by their followers. The public fancy built up men to match the task ahead. The facts of Daniel Boone's career are good enough for history, but they weren't good enough to satisfy the American imagination.

Daniel, for example, had trouble with the Indians, as other men commonly did. But in the stories made up about him, Daniel Boone could throw the Indians off his trail by swinging on grapevines, and if they shot at him he would, according to the legend, wait until he saw the flash of gunpowder and then dodge the bullet.

The real Daniel was probably lonely, as other men were. But the imaginary Daniel made a specialty of loneliness and called it the right to be by himself. He went into the deepest part of the forest, and when someone came along to settle within the sound of a rifleshot, he would shout, "Too crowded — too crowded! I want elbow room!" And he would move on.

The real men who were exploring big America became the heroes of heroic tales, told around the fireplace and the campfire. Yet even these heroes did not suffice for size. Still bigger characters had to be dreamed up. In various regions myth-men were conjured up to tackle the gigantic jobs that faced the people of the region.

Pecos Bill was the folk hero of the cowboys of the Southwest, including, of course, Texas. In Texas he had competition because of the size of the state itself. It was then the biggest state in the Union. Real Texas fans pointed out that if you took a piece of string and measured Texas from its northern border to its southern tip, then held the string at the top and moved the bottom end around, you would see that the length of Texas would stretch beyond Chicago.

So it would — and this seemed important to Texas. One Texan, wearing a ten-gallon hat, remarked to a crusty old Britisher, "You know, pardner, you could put England into Texas five times." To which the crusty old Britisher replied, "And to what purpose?"

To the Texan the fact that you could do it was purpose enough, but the fact of size did matter in many practical ways. Texas had the largest ranch in the world — and room for it. The ranch was the X.I.T. and it had three *million* acres when the average homestead in the nation was only 160 acres. When the west line of the ranch was fenced during the winter of 1885, the barbed wire ran for 200 miles. The distance was equal to that between New York and Washington, D. C., and the fence closed the border between the Texas Panhandle and the Territory of New Mexico. Such tremendous pasture had the advantages of flexibility. If the weather was severely cold in the north, the cattle could be driven south where it was warm.

Things were so big in the Southwest that the most improbable tales became real and it was only a short flight of fancy from such a real ranch and pasture to Pecos Bill. Being an American, he was the greatest cowboy of all time, and it need not surprise us that if Pecos Bill was troubled about the hundreds of cattle in his charge being restless when night

27

came, he would simply throw the loop of his lasso around the entire herd to keep them from stampeding. We are told that this care soothed the cattle so that "they slept like kittens."

To their folk gods Americans gave traits good and bad and values true and false that belonged to the people as a whole. And so, out of the way of life of men who cleared the land and hewed the forests, came Paul Bunyan. Paul triumphed over the continental land mass and changed the face of it as he moved about. You could always tell he had been there — wherever it was. When digging out Puget Sound in the Pacific Northwest he piled the dirt so high that the piles could be seen for miles, men said. One pile was named Mt. Ranier and another Mt. Baker.

The whole land was the playground of the hero of the lumberjacks. Paul roamed the forests from Maine to California, accompanied by Babe, his big Blue Ox, who made lakes with his hoofprints when he walked. Paul logged off North Dakota in a week and invented a cross-country saw that could cut down whole forests in a day. He revealed man's greed while showing his physical strength.

Paul was a big boss, too. So many men worked for him that some of them almost starved — waiting their turn to get into the dining room. Paul solved the problem by building lunch counters outside where his men could get light refreshments, such as steaks, while they worked their way up in the line for the regular chow. Inside the dining room the tables were so long that the waiters wore roller skates and they wore out three pairs while making the rounds with hot coffee. The salt and pepper wagon was driven by a midget and he usually drove the length of a table and stayed all night at the far end.

Almost always our humor has stretched out to take on the scale of a big country. In early Tennessee it was said that the land was so fertile that you could plant a pig's tail and grow a hog and that the fish were so aggressive that you didn't need a pole; in fact, you had to hide behind the trees to keep them from jumping into your arms.

28

Many size words were used to express favor or convey a compliment. If a man was generous, he was said to be bighearted. If he was very generous, he was said to have a heart as big as a rain barrel. A new enterprise or establishment was said to be bigger and better, as if being bigger made it necessarily better.

In a land of high mountains and deep valleys and immeasurable plains, we borrowed tall words from Latin and Greek and came up with words like *colossal* to picture something out of the ordinary, and we made many a small auditorium seem bigger by calling it a *colosseum*. We described the lowest and simplest models of our new cars with a French word that means the finest — *de luxe*. When the telephone was developed we coined the term long-distance for out-of-town calls. When superlatives ran out of meaning we came up with such terms as *super-colossal*. Actors became stars and little actors who hadn't made good and could hardly be seen were *starlets*. A play with a de luxe setting and a colossal cast came to be known as a *spectacular*.

Our habits of exaggeration linger on in the banter of rival regions and towns and states — as between Texas and Alaska. When Alaska was admitted to the Union, there was wide comment on the fact that the new state was more than twice as big as Texas, which used to be our biggest state. And the story went around that when a Texan objected an Alaskan retorted, "If you don't shut up, we'll divide into two states and then you'll be only the third largest state in the Union." The Texan is said to have answered back that if all the ice in Alaska melted, it would be the smallest state in the Union.

Another story goes that Macon, Georgia, once got tired of hearing the boasts of Atlanta and announced, although its rival was 500 miles from the coast, "If Atlanta could suck as hard as she could blow, she'd be a seaport."

The humor now is good, but the rivalry of regions was once grim and swelled into sectionalism. This sectionalism grew as the country grew.

In Washington's day "The West" meant along the Mississippi. By 1849 it meant along the Pacific.

Californians, far removed and with no fast means of travel, regarded the rest of the country as strange. They spoke of "going to the states" in much the same manner as the British spoke of "going out" to remote and less civilized colonies. How distinct and far away California felt in the 1850's is reflected in a popular song they sang:

> Oh, what was your name in the States —
> Was it Thompson or Johnson or Bates?
> Did you murder your wife
> And fly for your life?
> Say, what was your name in the States?

It was not the West, however, but the South that felt strong enough to organize itself into a separate country. The people of the South led a very different life from those in the North. Even their way of earning their daily bread differed. In much of the North, manufacturing prevailed; in the South, agriculture.

At first the South grew chiefly sugar cane, rice, tobacco, and cotton. The climate favored cotton, but picking the seeds out of it was such a slow process that a slave could clean hardly more than five or six pounds a day. Then in 1792 Eli Whitney, a young graduate of Yale University, went South to study law on a Georgia plantation. There he saw the need of a faster process of taking seeds out of cotton if the crop was to be profitable. Knowing something of mechanics from his father's metal-working shop in Massachusetts, Whitney invented an engine (in shorter form, a gin) which could clean the seeds from a thousand pounds of cotton in a day.

Mr. Whitney spent most of the money his invention brought in lawsuits trying to protect his patent. But the South made money out of the

gin. By 1829 Southerners were able to export more than $26,000,000 worth of cotton — half of all the exports of every kind sent out of the U.S.A. in that year.

As cotton grew to be the basis of the Southern plantation system, slave labor became more and more important to Southerners. Their concern was both economic and political. They were concerned not only with keeping slaves but also with the constitutional right of states to do so. And they were worried about being outvoted in Congress.

The population of the manufacturing North had grown by leaps and bounds as immigrants came in droves to seek jobs. The population of the South, on the other hand, grew only by natural increase. People in the North began to outnumber those in the South. As new states opposed to slavery came into the Union, Southern leaders began to fear that the South might be unable to keep any voice in national affairs unless it could extend the number of states where slavery was approved.

However, outcries against slavery, as well as declarations in favor of it, came from both the South and the North. Voices rose louder and louder on both sides of the issue. Some preached that slavery was "sin" and some praised it as "in the order of God." Antislavery groups fought among themselves. Some hoped for time in which to devise schemes that might gradually free the South of dependence on slave labor. Some demanded immediate action and, with the Massachusetts publisher, William Lloyd Garrison, denounced the Constitution for sanction of slavery. Garrison burned a copy of the Constitution on the Boston Common.

The argument was too hot for Congress. It passed a resolution that petitions submitted on either side of the issue were to be "laid upon the table and no further action shall be had thereon."

Against the furor arose a man with a plan. He was Senator Stephen A. Douglas of Illinois, affectionately known as the Little Giant because of his stocky build and his vigor in debate. Douglas suggested letting slavery alone where it existed and letting each new state decide for itself

whether to permit slavery or not. He advanced this idea in debates with Abraham Lincoln, who in 1858 was named by the newly formed Republican Party to run against Douglas for the Senate.

Lincoln's view was that, no matter where or how slavery was allowed, the institution of slavery was wrong, "a moral, a social, and a political wrong," and that the United States could not "endure permanently, half slave and half free." Douglas was elected by a narrow margin, but his "plan" satisfied neither the Southern plantation owners nor the Northern abolitionists. They both called him "Judas" and "traitor." Nevertheless, in 1860 he sought the Democratic nomination for President.

The Democratic Convention of that year opened in Charleston, South Carolina. The slavery issue split the delegates — those from eight states walked out — and no candidate was chosen. The Convention reassembled in Baltimore without the "bolters" and the "regulars" nominated Douglas. The bolters chose a candidate of their own — John Breckenridge of Kentucky.

The Republicans named Lincoln as their candidate and of course won the election, even though they failed to carry a single Southern state. It was a contest of territories. Early in February of the next year delegates from seven Southern states met to form the Confederate States of America.

In one of these states, South Carolina, was Fort Sumter, manned by a federal garrison of 83 men. On April 8, 1861, President Lincoln informed the Governor of South Carolina that he was sending food by ship to the garrison. The Governor of South Carolina ordered General Pierre G. T. Beauregard to demand the immediate surrender of the United States fort to the state. Major Robert Anderson, in command of Fort Sumter, refused. Beauregard fired on the fort with 50 cannons and so began the conflict known in the South as the War Between the States and in the North as the Civil War.

The end of the war came in 1865 but it didn't end the bitterness between North and South. Although the military terms set for the surrender of the South were generous, in the years that followed, Congress treated the South much as if it were a defeated foreign power. Distance prevented most people in the North from seeing with their own eyes how extreme were some of the measures of revenge.

But though size had sorely tried us, it would not be allowed to defeat us. Even while the war was dividing us north and south, men were setting about the task of connecting us east and west. We would conquer with rails the great distance between New York and the fabulous land of California.

Only a train pulled by a big steam engine and carrying passengers as well as freight would have the size and speed needed to link one side of the United States with the other. The stagecoach could make part of the distance — the 1,500 miles from Missouri to San Francisco — in seventeen days, but it carried little more than the baggage of the passengers.

In April 1860, the Overland Pony Express had begun runs between St. Joseph, Missouri, and San Francisco. The scheduled time was ten days, with carriers riding night and day and changing mounts every fifteen miles. It was spectacular speed for the distance and it brought great excitement. The first rider left St. Joseph on April 3 and when the last relay rider reached Sacramento on that trip, the California legislature adjourned and cannons boomed in honor of the event.

Here was progress of a sort. It was an improvement over the mails of a hundred years before. In 1760 there had been only eight mails a year between Philadelphia and the Potomac, and the pony rider in that day didn't have to set out until he had enough mail to make the trip pay. The Pony Express was at least regular, going each way once a week at breakneck speed. But the loads were light. They had to fit the saddlebags. That first rider carried only 49 letters and the postage was $5 for half an ounce. This was certainly no way to keep two sections of a great country in touch.

No, there had to be a railroad. Men had long talked of it, some idly, some seriously. Congress had even investigated and there was a big report in seven volumes. But now a man came along and talked of little else. He was a Connecticut-born engineer by the name of Theodore Dehone Judah, who had gone to California in 1855. He talked his idea of a transcontinental railroad so much that he came to be known as Crazy Judah.

But Judah was far from crazy. He knew what he was talking about. There must be a way to put a railroad across and around the granite crags of the range of mountains the Spanish had named saw-toothed: the Sierra Nevada. To prove his point, he went out and surveyed the route. Then, still talking, always talking, he went to Washington and laid his scheme before Congress and asked for action.

In October 1861 — three months after the defeat of the Northern forces at Bull Run by the Confederate Army — he succeeded. He was able to convince Congress that a transcontinental railroad was necessary to keep California and Nevada, with their rich gold deposits, in the Union. The railroad act, passed in 1862 at Judah's urging, provided big public funds to build the Central Pacific from Sacramento across the Sierra Nevada. In Utah, it would meet the Union Pacific, which would be built across Nebraska from Omaha.

The scheme was as wild as any ever given shape in legislative halls. Only in big America could it ever have been thought up, much less carried out. Judah died before the work was fairly commenced, but he had made the idea real and literally shown the way. The route followed by the builders varied little from the course he had surveyed.

Building the Central Pacific along this course was enough to cause dismay in the stoutest hearts. Iron rails weighing 85 pounds a yard had to be shipped from Pennsylvania all the 19,000 miles around Cape Horn at the tip of South America — or else carted across the Isthmus of Panama, since the canal there had not yet been built. The problems of engineering were beyond belief — and almost beyond achievement.

The rails would have to be laid in passes blasted through the granite of the Sierra Nevada. The lowest height at which a pass could be blasted was 7,000 feet. Gorges between precipices would have to be bridged or filled with millions of tons of dirt. And beyond the mountains lay hundreds of miles of desert, with no water for the railroad builders. Then more mountains — the Rockies.

When General William T. Sherman, a famous officer in the Northern army during the Civil War, heard of the plan to build this railroad, he said: "I would hate to buy a ticket on it for my grandchildren."

Sherman and other doubters reckoned without a 250-pound Paul Bunyan of a man named Charles Crocker, who had gone to California from Indiana at the age of twenty-six to seek his fortune. He found it. At the age of forty he undertook and saw through personally and daily a construction job that few believed possible.

Crocker met every problem the doubters and doomsters had foreseen. He even met and turned to triumph one that nobody had predicted. Near the beginning of the work, he ran out of workmen. Crocker sent to Sacramento and brought back 50 Chinese who had been living there. When his superintendent protested that these Chinese, weighing hardly more than 100 pounds, were no match for the task of carving through mountains, Crocker answered, "They built the Great Wall of China, didn't they?"

And they built the Central Pacific too. The first 50 made such an impression that Crocker hired 100 more in the next two days. Then he contracted to have boatloads brought out of the rice paddies of China. Ultimately the Chinese road builders numbered 15,000. Known as "Crocker's pets," they showed great teamwork as well as bravery and did the most hazardous part of the work as the railroad moved forward.

In seven years and against all the odds, Crocker and his pets laid an incredible thousand miles of track.

Meanwhile the Union Pacific nosed its way across Nebraska. By the winter of 1867 its tracks were in Cheyenne, Wyoming. During the Civil War its chief engineer, General Grenville M. Dodge, had had his own trouble getting manpower and he had imported bands of Irish immigrants. He had also advertised all over northern Europe for engineers and technicians who could help. After the war was over, men from both the Union and Confederate armies worked together at the job, and the two roads began to race toward each other. Construction was followed like a national sporting event today. Men wagered on whether the Chinese or the Irish would lay the greater mileage.

In the spring of 1869 the end of the job was in sight. Word reached Crocker that the crews of the Union Pacific had laid eight miles of track in a single day. Crocker offered to bet $10,000 that his Chinese could lay ten miles between daylight and dark. An official of the Union Pacific took the bet. Crocker planned his day carefully and placed spikes along the route. In twelve hours his Chinese, "working with the precision and grace of ballet dancers," laid ten miles of track with 56 feet added for good measure.

On May 10, 1869, the Central Pacific and the Union Pacific met at Promontory, Utah. A train from the Pacific Coast and a train from the East hove into sight at eleven in the morning, their whistles calling to each other as they approached. The locomotives, gaily decorated, stood almost nose to nose, separated only by a small space not yet bridged by track. A crew of Chinese brought forward the last ties and rails, and Leland Stanford, president of the Central Pacific, drove a spike of solid gold to finish the giant job. The telegraph sputtered the news to Washington and to San Francisco.

Again the giant had shown its stature and its power. Flesh and blood had done before men's eyes what the world might have expected that only Paul Bunyan, the American myth, could do. And the strength that had connected our coasts had been not only our own. East and West had met in the United States, not only in terms of our own geography, but also in terms of people from Asia and western Europe. That was something to think about.

So the railroads did more than unite parts of the country physically. They helped to unite it in feeling. Songs grew up to celebrate the railroad. They had an awareness of new experience and gave this new experience the lure of romance. In some of them there was gaiety and zest and the rhythm of the wheels upon the places where the rails joined, as in "Halleluja, I'm a Bum." There was humor — good American humor — celebrating the Irish in such songs as "Drill, Ye Tarriers, Drill":

> One day last week when the blast went off,
> A mile in the air went big Jim Gough.
> Well, the next time pay day came around,
> Big Jim a dollar short was found.

When he asked the reason why, Big Jim was told, "You were docked for the time you spent in the sky."

Part of the romance of the songs lay in the fact that a man need no longer feel he had to stay put. He could get up and go — fast. In "Lulu," the melody of which carries some of the loneliness of a train whistle on the prairie at night, a lovesick fellow working on the railroad is overcome by longing. He decides simply to lay down his sledge-hammer and hop a freight and go all the way across the country to see his long-haired gal.

Some of the songs glorified speed and made it seem almost sacred. Casey Jones was known as the greatest of the hoggers. (In railroad language engineers were called hogheads or hoggers). Casey was a hero because he was a speed king and always brought his train in On Time. In another song the man who heroically wrecked the Old '97 did it by going downgrade at 90 miles an hour. Something of the wild dash of the Pony Express was carried over to the Iron Horse, as the railroad was called.

The railroads were rife with romance also because they were a symbol of conquest, a further assurance that the settlers moving West could

46

really possess the land. This was an earlier conviction but now it was expressed in iron. Nothing would stand in the way — whether mountains or distance or Indians or buffalo.

Lust for land marked the white man's actions from the time he first set foot on these shores, and the size of the country had much to do with his lust and greed. There always appeared to be more and more land, and if the white man wanted either a particular parcel or a whole region, well, said he, the Indian could go somewhere else. To the settler it was that simple.

The farmers and merchants couldn't understand why the Indians, being hunters, wanted so much land anyway. "What is the right of the huntsman to the forest of a thousand miles over which he has ranged in quest of prey?" asked President John Quincy Adams in 1802. And fifteen years later President James Monroe declared, "The hunter or savage state requires a greater extent of territory to sustain it than is compatible with the progress and just claims of civilized life."

These statements put into official terms an attitude that had slowly hardened into a policy since the first settlements were founded. The earliest settlers had found the Indians not only friendly but neighborly and willing to live in peace. Powhatan, chief of the Pamunkeys in Virginia, gave the colonists at Jamestown corn and tobacco and came to their aid when they were in dire straits. Massasoit, chief of the Wampanoags in Massachusetts, gave the Pilgrims corn and venison during their first hard winter and then granted them land on which to raise their cattle.

But in both cases the whites wanted more of the plentiful land to put to their own use. The Indians, they said, could move back into the endless forests. Powhatan kept the peace in Virginia in spite of all the indignities visited upon his people and even after his daughter Pocahontas was kidnapped by the whites. But all the while the settlers kept encroaching upon the tribal lands of the Pamunkeys, clearing the forests and sowing fields of tobacco with seeds given them by the Indians.

After Powhatan's death his younger brother, Opechancanough, became chief of the Pamunkeys. Opechancanough had had enough. One day when he saw an Indian killed for "trespassing" on land a white man claimed without right, Opechancanough commenced what he intended to be a war of extermination, one that would drive the settlers back to their own native land if any survived. In one bloody day of stealth and fury, the Indians killed 347 people in settlements outside of Jamestown.

But Jamestown, seat of the government, survived. The white men planned their own war of extermination, and in due course they carried it out with treachery not matched by any Indian ruse. The governor of the colony, Sir Francis Wyatt, sent word to the Indians scattered in the woods that hostilities were at an end. The Indians accepted his word and returned to their homes. Then the whites fell upon them without warning and slaughtered them like animals. Opechancanough escaped the slaughter to lead his warriors again against the whites. When at last he was captured at the age of ninety he was shot in the back by one of the men appointed to guard him.

In New England the fate of the son of Massasoit was no less ghastly. Known as King Philip because of the dignity of his bearing, this chief led the Indians against the whites, and when he was finally captured his head was cut off and displayed as a trophy on a pole in Plymouth and left there for twenty years.

The pattern set by these early conflicts was repeated endlessly, with the scale increasing as the land unfolded. Solemn promises made at one time were ignored or broken at another. In 1832 President Andrew Jackson, who as a young man had acquired a great reputation as an Indian fighter, directed the removal of the entire Creek nation from its lands in Georgia. These lands had been guaranteed the Indians by a treaty between them and the United States in 1790. Claiming that the treaty couldn't be enforced, Jackson gave the Indians five years in which to move.

Before the period ended, however, some of the Indians showed signs of resistance and the removal was ordered immediately as a military measure. Those who resisted this order were handcuffed and put in chains and marched under escort all the way to Oklahoma. It was part of a forced migration of the Cherokee, the Chocktaw, and the Chickasaw, as well as the Creek, from land in the Southern states the white man wanted.

And it was the whole story of the American Indian in one tragic trek. The Indian could move on. It was a big country and there was plenty of everything for the taking. Plenty of game, for example, and especially buffalo. The plains were black with them.

One traveler tells of climbing a hill in Kansas from which he could see from six to ten miles in every direction. As far as the eye could see buffaloes were moving slowly north. The great herd took five days to pass a given point. In another case a herd took six weeks to cross the Arkansas River. The sight of these huge herds was overwhelming and so was the sound. "The pounding of their hoofs on the hard ground," said one frontiersman, "sounded like the roar of a mighty ocean, surging over the land and sweeping everything before it."

No wonder plainsmen thought there were enough shaggies to last forever! Reducing the herds would seem to be good riddance, for buffaloes certainly had no respect for modern improvements. They were barriers to trains. A train carrying the sculptor Bartholdi to California in 1871 was halted for five hours while a herd milled over the tracks, scornful of man and his wish for speed. There are many other earlier instances in which buffaloes blocked the passage of trains for hours at a time. Worse still, they were unfriendly to trains. At times they charged them from the side, breaking the couplings that linked the cars.

Steamboats fared no better. River traffic might be interrupted and passengers endangered while the herds swam the streams. On the upper Missouri, in 1867, buffaloes came so thickly in the path of a boat that the captain had to stop the engines and wait for hours while the beasts disentangled themselves from the wheel and stopped charging the sides of the boat.

The buffalo was not only a barrier to progress; he was also a rival in strength and size to the giant moving across the continent. A bull buffalo, standing six six feet tall at the shoulders, measuring twelve feet in length, weighing more than 4,000 pounds, was almost as big as Babe the Blue Ox. He was too big in numbers and size to let the giant pass uncontested.

So the slaughter began. At times the buffalo was slaughtered as any meat animal is slaughtered. Men became skilled at the job of shooting them for crews building the railroads and soldiers guarding the routes. One young marksman, William A. Cody, who later got himself known as Buffalo Bill, had a contract to supply the Kansas Pacific Railroad with twelve buffaloes a day, dressed and ready for the meat wagon. Once a small herd panicked and plunged into a gulch filled with snow. Cody shot all 55 in rapid succession.

In addition to systematic slaughter there was senseless slaughter, wanton and wasteful. Excursion trains ran in buffalo country and passengers took pot shots from the windows. Parties would go out to see how many tongues they could get; it was a great delicacy, the buffalo tongue. On one foray the winning party brought back twelve tongues, the losers eleven. Carcasses were left to rot.

In due course great stretches of buffalo country were covered with bleaching bones, so that the plains at times looked "white as from eternal frost." In 1886 there were estimated to be only 835 wild buffaloes left and these still subject to slaughter. Only as the herds neared extinction did men swing into action to preserve in some small measure what had been given us in such large measure. A leader in this effort was William Temple Hornady, who in 1882 was in charge of the collection of stuffed, mounted animals for the U. S. National Museum. An Indian

and a woman are also remembered among the few who saw the need to protect the vanishing buffalo.

The Indian's name was Walking Coyote. He roped two male and two female calves and set up in the West a breeding station where a purebred herd was raised. In Texas Mrs. Charles Goodnight persuaded her husband to protect a few calves on his cattle ranch. The buffaloes we see on reservations today or standing mangy or forlorn in amusement parks are descended from the few which were rescued in such fashion.

Women like Mrs. Goodnight, who, womanlike, thought of nurture instead of slaughter, began gradually to exercise a gentling influence on American life. This influence had been present from the beginning, but men had been so busy with conquest and with restlessly pushing back the frontier that they had given women little chance to mold affairs beyond the home and fireside.

Women had come to Jamestown in 1620 — two years before the dreadful war with Opechancanough broke out. The women who came were known as Tobacco Brides because any man who wanted to woo and win one as a wife had to have 120 pounds of tobacco before he was even considered eligible by those who governed the colony. Other Tobacco Brides had come later to Virginia. The Pilgrims had come in families to Plymouth, but of the eighteen wives who arrived on the *Mayflower* only five survived the first winter. Ten years later — in 1630 — Puritan families swarmed by the thousands into Massachusetts Bay.

Never before had men and women worked in partnership on so vast a scale. The opening up of America brought a new dignity to women and prepared the way for a new respect. To be sure, they were given no part in the councils of government at first. Even the remarkable Constitution of the United States didn't recognize women as citizens. But by the time the movement to the West mounted toward its climax, the giant's wife had to be recognized. She had shown bravery and toughness in colonial days and in early migrations along the frontier, but she showed these qualities in new abundance as the settlers moved to the far West.

The worst disaster of the movement West came in 1846 when the Donner Party — a group of families from Illinois and Iowa — were caught in the snows of the Sierra Nevada. Most of the party perished; it was Mrs. Tamsen Donner who survived long enough to take her three daughters to meet a rescue party. Then she walked back five miles to die with her husband, who was too weak to travel.

Tamsen Donner was carrying school books with her on that trip to California. She was going to see that her children and other children were taught. Women carried westward the seeds of learning. They encouraged reading and talking and all the things that make for what we call culture.

They carried manners and graces, too. When Fred Harvey got a concession to serve meals at wayside houses on the Atchison, Topeka & Santa Fe Rail Road, completed in 1883, he invited attractive young women to serve as waitresses. They flocked West in droves and immediately their presence lent tone and atmosphere to the eating places. If a man came in without a coat there was a sleek alpaca coat hanging just inside the door and he could put it on, along with a tie hanging there also, if he wanted to eat in a Harvey House.

It was out where the West begins that women of the U.S.A. first got rights as citizens. In 1869 the Territory of Wyoming passed laws giving women the right to vote and hold office and leave property in their wills. When Wyoming joined the Union in 1890 the law stood and Wyoming became the first state to grant such rights to women. Another Western state, Colorado, granted them in 1893 and two others, Utah and Idaho, in 1896.

New influences began to work upon the giant. Not all of them, of course, were feminine. Part of the change was simply a matter of growing up, of using brains as well as brawn. Men were used to doing things by muscle power. Then along came the machine. At first the machine

58

didn't seem to be a threat to the American. An engine on a track, with a man in control of it, was all right. It carried him and didn't compete with him. It competed with horses. But the engine that came along and promised to do a man's job better than he — in fact better than lots of men working together — well, that was quite another matter.

Came the steam drill, for example, for boring holes in rocks to plant explosives. This work had been done by powerful and skilled men who hammered holes into rocks with iron and then later steel rods. The steam drill promised to do the work better and faster and with almost no effort on the part of the man.

Here was something to be greeted with suspicion. The steam drill was offered to Charlie Crocker toward the end of his gigantic job of drilling through the mountains of the West. He turned it down. But when from 1870 to 1873 the Chesapeake and Ohio Rail Road drove its Big Bend tunnel through the Alleghenies in West Virginia, the steam drill came into use.

A showdown between man and the machine was now certain and the heavyweight contest created another American myth-hero: John Henry, the steel-drivin' man of the railroads. In men's minds and as their champion he was given some of the dimensions of Paul Bunyan. In most popular versions of his story and in the folk song about him, he was a Negro giant, overpowering in strength from the hour of his birth. Before he was seven weeks old he found a piece of steel and his pappy's hammer and broke big stones while his folks were at church. When they came home, John Henry was working on the biggest stone of all and singing at the top of his lusty voice as he struck each blow:

> If I die (WHAM!)
> A railroad man (WHAM!)
> O bury me (WHAM!)
> Under the sand (WHAM!)
> With a pick and shovel (WHAM!)
> At my head and feet (WHAM!)
> And a twenty-pound hammer (WHAM!)
> In my hand. (WHAM!)

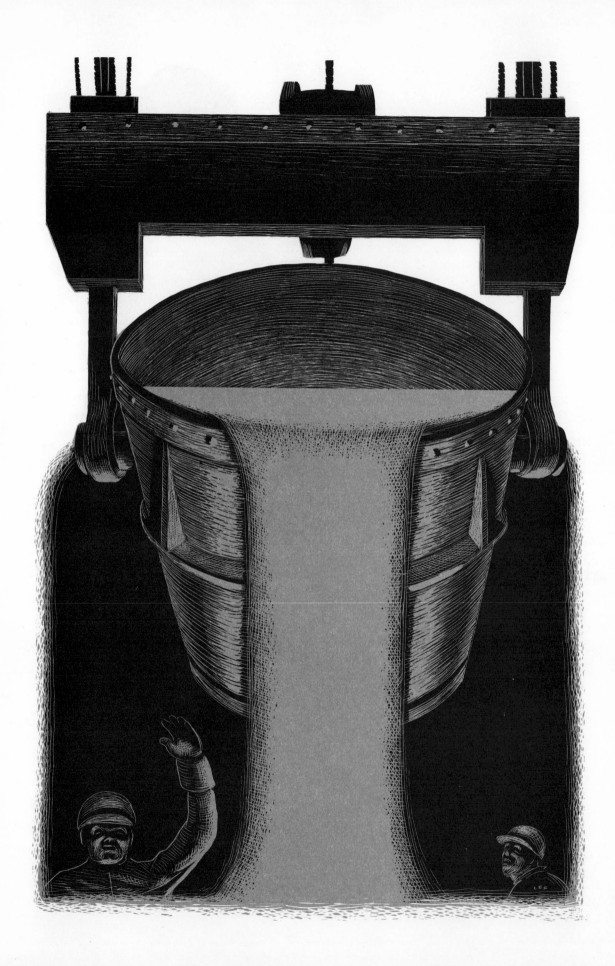

This was the lad who grew up to fight man's battle against the steam drill, hoping to silence its threat to the American. In that contest he fought for nine long hours. And he won! With powerful blows he drilled more holes than the steam drill and drilled them faster. But in the ninth hour the spectators could see John Henry show fatigue. At the end he was exhausted. He beat the drill but he died — with his hammer in his hands.

The story of John Henry spread through the land, growing as it went, changing color, adapting itself to local circumstances. Its spread was a kind of acknowledgment that man had met his match, no matter how big and strong he was.

If you can't lick 'em, join 'em. So runs the old adage. After all, man had created the machine. The next step was to get smart about it and put it to daily work in man's service. To do this would challenge the imagination as much as would any great task ahead. The mastery grew —slowly but in dozens of ways — so that America became stronger physically than it had ever been before.

You can probably get the story best in steel. Sixty years ago much of the work in steel mills was done by hand — and very awkwardly. When a loaded iron ore vessel drew alongside a dock at a steel plant, a great basketlike contraption called a staging was lowered into the hold of the ship and men shoveled into the staging the iron ore from which the steel was to be made. Then the staging was slowly drawn up through a hatch and swung out on the pier. Men shoveled the ore into wheelbarrows and wheeled it to the furnaces.

One day a man named George Hulett watched this process and figured that it was no way to feed hungry furnaces that would make steel for the nation's growing needs. If the steel industry were to grow, too, it must have big machines to help the hands. On a scrap of paper Hulett sketched out the first plans for a huge ship-unloading machine that today does in twenty minutes what it used to take all week to do.

Go to a big steel plant such as Bethlehem Steel Company's Lacka-

wanna Plant near Buffalo, New York. Watch an ore vessel tie up and see four Hulett-type unloaders go majestically to work. Standing 100 feet high and running on tracks, they move toward the ore vessel. The unloader's great neck stretches out like a dinosaur's. A scoop at the end of it opens like a great mouth and seizes 16 tons in one bite. Then the unloader glides back along its track and drops the ore onto a belt that takes it where it's needed.

There is regularity and rhythm about the operation. One can almost think of a work song to go along with the job. John Henry saw this monster coming and he fought it and tried to outdo it. But the kind of imagination that created the John Henry myth created the unloader and showed how, in a land where all is big and must be forever bigger, man can have his strength multiplied a thousandfold.

It must be remembered that the U.S.A. grew to fullness at the very time when new and hitherto unknown sources of energy were coming into wide use. First coal, then oil, then electricity, then the promise of the atom. The result is that, during the past 75 years, a sense of strength from power has joined our feeling of strength from size. In a word, we felt bigger than ever when we found out how strong we were.

Throughout it all we have remained conscious of distance. Four of our greatest industries have had to do with going places and going as fast as possible.

We built railroads like mad. One route to the Pacific wasn't enough. By 1893 we had four. With side lines these four had enough track to reach almost around the earth. And still we weren't content. We kept right on building and we kept improving the lines we had built, chiefly to make it safe for the trains to go faster. The first steel rails used in 1865 weighed 50 pounds to the yard. By 1900 they were twice as heavy and by 1916 they weighed 130 pounds to the yard. With crushed rock for ballast under the heavy rails, trains could go at higher speeds and with more comfort.

Railroads launched great fleets of luxury trains with names like the

Cannon Ball and the Katy Flyer that conjured speed. Trains were put into operation that went long distances without stopping at small stations along the way. They were called Limiteds, having only a limited number of stops. The most famous of all, the Twentieth Century Limited, inaugurated in 1902, ran the whole distance of almost 1,000 miles between Chicago and New York without a scheduled stop. Bragged of as "the Greatest Train in the World," it occasionally reached the incredible speed of 100 miles per hour. Gradually, as the whole roadbed improved, the Twentieth Century cut its running time from twenty hours to eighteen and then sixteen. It seemed almost to get up and leave the rails.

Yet trains were not enough. We wanted automobiles as big as Conestoga wagons, automobiles that could cross mountain ranges without half trying and go like lightning on open stretches. We wanted a machine for eating distance and we wanted it under our personal control. We wanted to be able to go where we wanted to go at the moment and not have to go just where the trains went.

To move around in the way the land encouraged us to, we needed not only automobiles but also interlacing roads. The two went hand in hand and the growth of roads was even more exciting than the growth of automobiles. We put up signs showing how to get from town to town and then hit upon the idea of highways with signs showing how to get to distant towns. The lure of the far-off was all the bigger for being made to seem close at hand. At least you could say in a small town that you lived on the road to . . . and it seemed to bring the place closer.

Maps began coming out of Detroit, where most of the automobiles were manufactured. For regions where road signs had not been put up, instructions in guidebooks for motorists might read, "Turn right at the schoolhouse, then left at the cowpens." Not until 1912 was it seriously suggested that there might be a national highway that would go all the way across the country. In that year the idea was put forward with vigor

by Carl Fisher, a young man who had earned millions by making a headlight that would enable cars to travel at night.

Fisher proposed that the automobile industry build the transcontinental road and profit by the impulse it would give to the building of good roads everywhere. With all the arts of salesmanship, he set about putting the idea across. It would be called the Lincoln Memorial Highway. A red, white and blue insignia with a prominent L appeared as its symbol. Highway memberships were sold and President Wilson — the last President to drive to his inauguration in a horse-drawn carriage — bought the first membership.

To explore part of the route, a caravan of cars of all makes started out from Indianapolis for Los Angeles in July 1913. With many a mishap but without a major disaster, the caravan made Los Angeles in 34 days.

It was a good thing that the drivers were experts. Not only did they have to cross unbridged streams but they drove the whole distance on impossible roads. There were miles and miles of paved streets in cities, but at the time Fisher made his daring suggestion and the caravan took off there was only one mile of paved public road outside of city limits in the entire country. That was near Detroit.

Not until 1928 were the permanent markers of the Highway placed. Working from morning to night on a September day in that year, hundreds of Boy Scouts across the country dug holes and set 4,000 concrete posts with signs to show the road from the West Coast to New York.

Meanwhile, the construction of the Highway had helped give the impulse to road building which Fisher had predicted. Roads were paved by the hundreds, then the thousands, and then by the hundreds of thousands of miles. By 1925 driving on good roads had become a habit in many parts of the country. But still motorists and truckers and bus companies weren't content. There was cross traffic in and near towns and every now and then drivers had to slow down. So highways were followed by superhighways with bridges above them for cross traffic.

Sometimes the superhighways were called turnpikes after the old practice of laying across the road a pike or spear which was turned up after you had paid a toll.

The first great superhighway was the Pennsylvania Turnpike. When the first section of it was finished and opened in 1940, a motorist could drive 217 miles from Harrisburg to Pittsburgh without a single interruption. On his way he passed through some of the Allegheny Mountain tunnels drilled by crews building the old South Penn Railroad, abandoned in 1885. Other tunnels were bored through the mountains by the crews of the Turnpike itself.

There began a new era of highway building of which the end is not yet in sight. Today we are engaged in building 41,000 miles of superhighways to be finished in 1973. We call the equipment we are using to do it earth-moving machinery. We have set out literally to change the face of the earth.

Here again, as in the case of the device for speeding up the unloading of iron ore in the steel industry, a man used his head to get the basic idea of how to do it. The basic idea was a treadmill, a revolving metal track, attached instead of wheels to machines that needed tremendous power to push or pull. The man who thought up the treadmill idea for machines was Benjamin Holt of Stockton, California, and the year was 1885. With a gasoline engine available for power, the world was ready for its first Caterpillar tractor, which came along in 1904. With treadmills on both sides, the tractor inched along like the well-organized worm that bears the same name.

Power than can be used in valleys or on hills, in any and all the crazy circumstances a road builder may meet, came with the Caterpillar. When it doesn't do all the work itself it makes it possible for other machines to play their part. For example, one writer tells of seeing a huge scraper used to scale down a 500-foot hill. The scraper is a powerful thing in itself and can do the work of a thousand men with dynamite and wheelbarrows. It chews down a hill from the top, but it takes a

Caterpillar to pull the scraper to the top in the first place. So as we moved mountains and mastered that part of nature that got in our way, Paul Bunyan came back to life in a machine. He hadn't been such a myth after all.

Not the spectacle of any one machine, however, but the performance of a great army of them and their effect on the landscape give us a picture of our ability to change environment through power. This is an ability we have shown over and over again. It creates in us a habit of making big changes and of thinking that no change is too big to make.

An engineering journal, writing of the bridge being built to span the Narrows at the entrance to the harbor of New York City, said: "Everything about the Narrows bridge is big, bigger or biggest." The journal wasn't exaggerating. The twelve-lane Narrows bridge was planned as the longest in the world.

But all the railroads and highways and bridges couldn't cut distance enough to suit us. We had a feeling that only the flying machine with increasingly increasing speeds could do it.

On the morning of December 17, 1903, the flying machine had become a fact — an American fact. From the sands near Kitty Hawk, North Carolina, Orville Wright made the first flight in a machine heavier than air that used power to stay aloft. There were four flights that morning, two for Orville and two for Wilbur. On the first flight the plane rose only ten feet from the ground and the flight lasted only twelve seconds. But the important thing was that the plane lasted; it was brought safely back to earth to fly again. Gradually the flights that day increased in height and distance. On the fourth flight the plane rose 852 feet above the earth and flew half a mile — in 59 seconds.

The progress made in this one day showed how the speed of the flying machine might become the next means to do away with distance.

By 1950 planes carrying fifty passengers flew across the continent. They were not "limited." We had made up a new term for timetables, a

very American term: non-stop. Within a hundred years after the Pony Express was taking ten days to carry mail from Missouri to California we were carting passengers and freight all the way from New York to California in eight hours. But it needn't take that long. The turbojet, a new type of engine that enabled airplanes to go faster and higher with heavier loads, had been worked out by an Englishman named Frank Whittle.

Whittle had spent much of his boyhood making model planes and dreaming of improved design. He had noticed that when the air in a toy balloon is released suddenly, the balloon is thrust upward by the released air. Why couldn't a motor be designed to use this principle of thrust? As a young man, Whittle worked his theory out on paper and patented it. By 1936 there was a small jet company in Great Britain that he was in on. By the end of World War II the turbojet for fighter planes was in production. After the war the jet engine was installed on transport planes and by 1951 the British had jets in passenger service. British jets were the first to fly the Atlantic.

However, the first jets weren't big enough to suit American airlines. They weren't big enough to cross non-stop from London or Paris to New York, except when aided by favorable winds. The American lines began insisting that airplane manufacturers make a big jump in size and design and build planes that would carry 140 passengers — three times as many as the earlier jets — and carry them twice as far. The new planes must cover distances of three or four thousand miles. The Boeing Company, out in the Paul Bunyan country, was the first to respond.

On January 25, 1959, one of these giant jets, built by Boeing and flown by American Airlines, carried 112 passengers on its first non-stop flight across the country from Los Angeles to New York in record time: four hours and three minutes. Fifty-six years after the first hesitant Wright flight, the U.S.A. had jets plying the skies over the oceans, bringing Paris as close to New York by air as Washington, D. C., is to New York by car.

To fill the big jets with passengers, economy rates were introduced. The bigness of the planes and the smaller fares meant flight for the masses — for more and more people. By carrying many passengers, planes could carry them at lower rates. Here was one of many cases where our feeling for bigness led to benefits for a great number of people. Back of much of our mass production is the thought of goods for everybody and everybody's good.

With such stupendous strides in physical development, Americans are tempted to think of the U.S.A. as a powerhouse. During World War II, we described ourselves as "the arsenal of democracy." We coined the phrase because, before we entered the war, we were supplying Britain and France with arms. We count our resources in physical terms, in terms of size and strength that can be seen and measured with numerals. This habit sometimes makes us seem to our friends pretty cocky.

For instance, some of us have boasted that in World War II our might saved Europe from the armies of the Nazi dictator, Hitler. The point of view of the British is that *they* saved *us,* by fighting Nazi Germany for two years before we did, thus giving us time to build up our armed forces.

Usually when we brag, we are just trying to tell how good we would like to think we are or would like to be. We should remember, perhaps, that the word *brag,* although it has an American twang, is, in Old French, akin to the word "bray."

There are good reasons, all of them plain to see, for taking pride in what we have done. Nevertheless, it's well for us also to remember that some of the hidden sources of our power may be as important as those that are visible. Our nation grew up as a child of the civilized world and, while growing, was blessed with a great deal of help from other nations. This foreign aid was always present, even though it didn't show itself in forms that citizens could readily grasp.

There was, for one thing, Great Britain's backing of the Monroe

Doctrine. Announced by President James Monroe in his message to Congress in December of 1823, this Doctrine stated that European powers must keep their hands off the New World. It was an American declaration, but the proposal had been made two years earlier by Foreign Minister George Canning of Great Britain, and it was clearly understood that the British Navy, which then ruled the waves, would help enforce the Doctrine.

Through the Monroe Doctrine and because of the distance of our country from other countries that might prove hostile, we were able to go all the way up to our entry into World War I on April 7, 1917, without spending more than a tiny bit of our income to defend ourselves in foreign wars. At the most important period of our expansion we didn't have to maintain any huge armed forces. Nothing to speak of was diverted from peaceful purposes. In this good fortune we were unique among the great nations.

In another way, too, through its bigness, the U.S.A. received benefits from the Old World. America admitted many people from many lands to its benefits and was in turn blessed by them.

Following the habit of hospitality on the frontier, where an extra plate was often set at the table just in case somebody might come, America set millions of extra plates. There was land for all, food for all, room for all. Why shut the door on those who wanted to come and share our good fortune?

We did in due course shut the door. And there was ill will at times toward the newcomers. But by and large we not only received them in droves but also continued to invite and welcome them. Big America became known throughout the world as a sanctuary, a place of refuge for those who would flee tyranny. It was an American woman of Jewish faith, Emma Lazarus, who wrote the words on the base of the Statue of Liberty that sum up the gentleness of the giant:

78

Give me your tired, your poor,
Your huddled masses yearning to breathe free,
The wretched refuse of your teeming shore,
Send these, the homeless, tempest-tost to me;
I lift my lamp beside the golden door.

One great church with Old World connections but with the spirit of the New added this petition to its Book of Common Prayer: "Defend our liberties and fashion into one united people the multitudes brought hither out of many kindreds and tongues."

This came to pass. Here you find the Shaunneseys, the Smiths, the Stanislowskis, the Schultzes, the Sadis, the Wallaces, the Rosenfields and the Monets — all living in one block, all reflecting different ways of life in the process of being made one. And the land, being big enough to receive the multitudes, has been made bigger still and stronger still by the skills and talents and variety of experience the multitudes brought.

So the giant U.S.A. found itself more and more in contact with the people and the nations of the world. As it had grown at home in size and strength, so now it began to grow in international spirit. Its idealism struggled to match its sense of power. In two World Wars, it was called upon to use this power cooperatively with other nations to protect them and itself from threatening tyrants. After World War II, much of Europe lay in bomb-shattered ruins. By contrast, no bomb had touched the U.S.A. Not only was it intact but it had most of the world's wealth. Then it realized for the first time how big and important was its mission. It began a program of aid to other countries such as history had not seen before.

Already we had what was, for a young nation, a long tradition of philanthropy — a big word with a bigger meaning: the love of humanity. In 1889 one of our richest men, Andrew Carnegie, developed what he called a Gospel of Wealth. "A man who dies rich dies disgraced," he said. His money came from steel, the sinews of a growing industrial country. By the time Carnegie died in 1919 his gifts amounted to $350,000,000 — 23 times as much as the cost of the whole Louisiana Purchase.

John D. Rockefeller made his money from oil. Even as a young man he had a habit of giving to worthy purposes more than $1,000 a year. By the time of his death in 1937 he had given away half a billion dollars. John D. Rockefeller, Jr., until his death in 1960, spent much of his time spending money for good causes and managing the charitable funds set up by his father. These funds include the Rockefeller Foundation, established in 1913 *to promote the well-being of mankind throughout the world."*

Many of the gifts of our philanthropists and churches went to help people in far places, thus linking us with the rest of the world. The story of the Ford Foundation, now the largest of all, shows how the interests of American giving have widened. Established by automobile manufacturer Henry Ford in 1936, its aid was at first confined to projects in Michigan, where Mr. Ford had made his money and felt at home. Enlarged in 1950, it launched upon a program that touched every inhabited continent of the world.

It turns out that we did have a heart as big as a rain barrel! And a good thing, too, for by the summer of 1947, two years after the end of World War II, it was plain that only the vast wealth of the United States could restore Europe. The amounts needed would have to come from government — they would be far greater than private funds could supply.

It was then that Secretary of State George Marshall made a commencement address at Harvard University, saying that if the states of Europe would get together and plan to work together to rebuild their lands, the United States would help through great gifts and loans. By the summer of 1948 Congress had set aside five *billion* dollars as a first offering toward a comeback for Europe.

The whole program of aid came to be known as the Marshall Plan

after the man who first publicly proposed it. The Soviet Union refused to enter the scheme and told the countries it controlled to stay out. Even so, eighteen western and southern European nations joined together to benefit from the Plan. As a condition of receiving aid, each agreed not only to work hard for itself but also to work with the others.

Thus the giant U.S.A. showed that it had strength to spare in peace as well as war. In fact, it showed in time that it had enough strength to help create a rival, a giant of almost equal size in wealth and population. Eight years after the Marshall Plan had drawn together European nations that had been quarreling for centuries, six of them — France, West Germany, Holland, Belgium, Italy and Luxembourg — signed a very new type of treaty for Europe. In the Treaty of Rome in 1955, the six agreed to work as closely together in matters of trade as if they were in effect a group of united states.

They agreed, in time, to do away entirely with taxes and limits on goods sold across their borders and to reduce these restrictions at once. They allowed a free movement of laborers from one country to another as needed. They set up a common executive and a common parliament. They called themselves the European Economic Community and they came commonly to be called the Common Market. By 1962 their population was 170,000,000 strong and they were making almost as much of John Henry's steel as the U.S.A.

The Common Market is not the only new giant at large today. The Soviet Union is one that is at the stage of throwing its weight around and blustering and sometimes breathing fire like a dragon. China may prove to be a bigger dragon still. Africa is growing in stature and energy. As more countries learn to capture and use nuclear energy, its power may create still more giants, even create them out of pygmies.

How we shall work with the new kind of world being created before our eyes, no one can say. Our deep, undying sense of size continues to influence our ideas and our actions. The U.S.A. looks upon itself as the champ; it has never been defeated — never even been knocked down, much less knocked out. But can the champ deal with today's new circumstances alone or does it need to become a partner in something still bigger?

In a series of lectures at Harvard University in 1962, Governor Nelson A. Rockefeller of New York saw the hope of the free world's future in the kind of federalism we invented when we formed the U.S.A. On July 4, 1962, the President of the United States, John F. Kennedy, made a speech at Independence Hall, Philadelphia. He spoke of our *interdependence* with the Common Market countries and said that we should "be prepared to discuss with a United Europe the ways and means of forming a concrete Atlantic partnership, a mutually beneficial partnership, between the new union now emerging in Europe and the old American union founded here 175 years ago."

For a long time other thoughtful Americans have been suggesting some form of partnership. One of the first was Clarence Streit, whom *Time* magazine called "the prophet from Missoula." Having grown up in Missoula, Montana, Streit became correspondent for *The New York Times* in Geneva, Switzerland, at the time of the League of Nations — the U.N.'s forerunner. In 1941, he proposed a Declaration of Interdependence which would unite the democracies of Europe and North America.

Although Streit was never known as "Crazy Clarence," in the fashion of Judah, his early ideas received at best a brush-off. But Streit refused to be discouraged. He gave up newspapering and devoted his life to writing and speaking and forming committees to work for what he called "Atlantic Union." Today you can often read his phrase — without quotes — on the front pages of your newspaper.

Whatever the American people decide about joining some larger union, it is good for us to reckon not only with the things, but also with the ideas that have grown from our habit of bigness. We are more than our machines and more than a machine.

In developing our ideas we had a great advantage: We had no old and fixed culture to overcome or replace on these shores. Other giants like Russia and China must spend a lot of energy getting rid of their past. We were able to create anew and we had the space and resources to do it on a grand scale. Geography and plenty put new notions in our heads. Nothing was too good for anybody. This is an American idea, pure and simple, and it is precious.

It shows up in the way we have thought about education. The very idea that *every* child in a vast and untutored land should have a chance at formal schooling was an idea no less dramatic and imaginative than that of joining the East and West by railroad. It is simply in another realm and it has been carried out so gradually and with such acceptance that we still aren't aware of how stupendous it is.

To see this idea in its true dimensions you would have to trace it back to Horace Mann, a Massachusetts legislator and educator in the first half of the nineteenth century. Then you would have to watch the idea unfold in our history. But you can see it indirectly when you realize how far we have already gone beyond it. For now the belief prevails, for the first time in history, that every young man and woman should have a *college* education. This notion is so big and dumfounding that it vexes some people. But there it is, right in the middle of our planning, unfolding logically out of our past. Whatever you think of the proposition, you can't ignore it any more than you could have ignored Crazy Judah.

We will go on with our physical achievements. That's for sure. We can't stop. We can't let mountains or well enough alone. We will play cowboy in outer space and continue mastering our environment. But gradually we may discover that bigness is more than size and that what is within us has dimensions of the spirit as great as any feats of conquest.

Consider the story of John V. Farwell. If there were such a person as a typical American, this man would qualify. Son of a merchant, he went from New York with his family in a covered wagon at the age of

86

thirteen to a squatter's homestead about 100 miles from Chicago. At nineteen, with $3.45 in his pocket, John went to that city to make his fortune. He made it. By 1864, when he was thirty-nine, Farwell was head of a big store called Farwell, Field & Company.

The next year Marshall Field withdrew to go into business for himself, but Farwell, believing in the future of Chicago and the country, expanded. By 1869 he had built a new store with many floors and a steam-powered elevator. The next year the building burned. Farwell built it back bigger and taller than ever and put in a steam-powered elevator larger and taller than the one before. Along came the Great Fire of 1871 and burned this new building down too.

Not only Farwell's store but all Chicago stores and virtually the whole city lay in ashes. Of course Chicago would rebuild, but it was talked around the country and the world that Chicago merchants would ask that their debts be forgiven as one means of getting started again.

A meeting of merchants was held. Farwell, who had been twice burned out, was the first to speak. He rose and said that his firm would pay every debt, dollar for dollar. He hesitated a moment, then added: "And with interest."

Farwell was a merchant prince who made good in what we have come to think of as usual American fashion. He owned part of the vast X.I.T. ranch in Texas. He had achieved the sort of business success we commonly celebrate. But he never did anything bigger than he did when he announced in simple terms that his behavior would be as big as his business.

How our country will develop in the future depends on others as well as us, but, if we may judge by our heritage, much will depend on the size of our ideas and imagination. Whatever we do, we'll do it in a big way.

And with interest.

GETTING TO KNOW MORE

If you think, after reading this book, that the U.S.A. is big, you ought to see the literature about it. And you will want to. Our history is full of fascinating detail. Getting to know more and more about what interests you most will afford you a lifetime of reading pleasure.

A friend of mine who has flown a small airplane over many parts of the world tells me that it is surprising how much one can learn about a country from the air. It is at least a good introduction, but every now and then you see something that makes you want to put down and investigate.

Let me tell you now, after the aerial view you have had from reading this book, some of the books and articles that helped me most in writing it.

The West looms large in any account of American life, so let's begin with that. *Men to Match My Mountains* by Irving Stone has the imagination and scope and spirit that ought to go along with a book on the opening of the West. *The Big Four* by Oscar Lewis gives a grand account of Theodore Judah and of the men responsible for financing and sponsoring the Central Pacific Railroad on its way to join the Union Pacific. *Railroads in the Days of Steam* by Albert L. McCready in consultation with Lawrence W. Sagle has some good pictures and a lot of picturesque detail. An informative booklet, *The Railroad Rail: Raw Materials to Right-of-Way,* is issued by the Bethlehem Steel Company. And for your listening pleasure I can certainly recommend a record, *Songs of the Railroad* by the Merrill Jay Singers, arranged by Jimmy Leyden.

Good books on Indians are plentiful. I found the following of chief interest for my story: *Indians on the Warpath* by David C. Cooke; *The American Heritage Book of Indians,* with narrative by William Brandon; *Indian Wars and Warriors — West* by Paul I. Wellman; and *The Seminoles* by Edwin C. McReynolds.

For a narrative of the Donner disaster, see George R. Stewart's *Ordeal by Hunger,* and for an excellent short account, see "Epic of Endurance" by Fairfax Downey, *Reader's Digest* for October 1939.

Cattle Empire by Lewis Nordyke gives you the story of the fabulous X.I.T. ranch. A quick picture of the Pony Express is painted by John Bach McMaster in his *A History of the People of the United States from the Revolution to the Civil War.*

The ghastly slaughter of the buffalo is graphically narrated by Wayne Gard in *The Great Buffalo Hunt.* Mari Sandoz gives further details obtained from a careful study of early records in two books, *The Buffalo Hunters* and *Love Song to the Plains.* A compact review of the buffalo and his plight will be found in "Old Man Buffalo" by Donald Culross Peattie, which appeared in *Natural History* for October 1943 and in *Reader's Digest* for November 1943.

"What Wyoming Did for Women" by Paul Friggens, in *Reader's Digest* for September 1960, offers a good summary of the circumstances that led to granting women the vote for the first time.

Usually firsthand or eyewitness reports of events are the most interesting and reliable material of history, whatever period you are reading about.

Allen Nevins and Henry Steele Commager have edited a fine volume of firsthand accounts called *The Heritage of America.* It includes, for example, the observations of Mr. Birkbeck from which I quoted on page 16. In *The Spirit of Seventy-Six* Mr. Commager has presented the story of the American Revolution as told by those who took part in it. And *The American Rebellion* by Sir Henry Clinton presents in Clinton's own words — thousands of them — the British side of the American Revolution as well as Clinton's view of Cornwallis and other associates.

Living Ideas in America, edited with commentary by Henry Steele Commager, brings you 200 documents and papers that touch on various phases of American culture and policy. Here are Horace Mann's views on universal education, excerpts from President Monroe's message to Congress stating the doctrine that bears his name, and General George C. Marshall's Harvard University address in which he put forward the United States plan for aid to Europe after World War II.

A paperback handy to have around is *American Historical Documents,* edited by Harold C. Syrett. And a remarkable and convenient collection of excerpts from books that reflect the development of American life and thought has been issued by the U. S. Government Printing Office: *A Guide to the Study of the United States of America.*

Next in reliability to firsthand accounts of events by persons involved in them are books and articles based on a close study of these accounts. Alice Morse Earle has interesting stuff in her book, *Home Life in Colonial Days,* including a good description of the Conestoga wagon. *Women's Life and Work in the Southern Colonies* by Julia Cherry Spruill tells of the Tobacco Brides in Jamestown and pictures many details in the home life of early America. You can get the background of the celebrated statue at the entrance of New York Harbor in *Bartholdi and the Statue of Liberty* by Willadene Price.

There are histories of American life to suit every taste and purpose. Some cover in broad strokes the whole period of our development. For example, *The First Book of American History* by Henry Steele Commager begins with the discovery of the New World and brings you up to the present. But in general the histories that cover short periods have more time for the convincing detail that makes a story real. In *A History of the United States from the Compromise of 1850 to the Final Restoration of Home Rule in the South in 1877,* James Ford Rhodes takes four volumes to tell about a period that lasts only 27 years.

Some of my friends have written about aviation with a wealth of information. Among them are Wolfgang Langewiesche, author of the classic on the art of flying, *Stick and Rudder,* and Robert N. Buck, who pilots intercontinental jets and has written on aviation for popular magazines and for *Air Facts,* a journal for pilots. *The Saga of Flight,* an anthology edited by Neville Duke and Edward Lanchbery, contains stories by persons who have experienced the excitement of flight. It includes the brief report by Wilbur and Orville Wright of their first flights at Kitty Hawk.

Two sprightly magazine articles provide a good deal of information on highways and highway building: "The Lincoln Highway: An Epic in Automobile History" by Elizabeth Fagg Olds, appearing in *True* for September 1957, and "They're Changing the Face of the Earth" by Hubert Kelley in *Nation's Business* for October 1954 and *Reader's Digest* for January 1955.

There are several good books about American folklore. I found Walter Blair's *Tall Tale America* to be the most useful. Others include *Pecos Bill, The Greatest Cowboy of All Time* by James C. Bowman and Dell J. McCormick's *Tall Timber Tales.*

A handy book to keep you straight on dates and pull together into some sort of order the hundreds of events that make up the story of our common life is the *Encyclopedia of American History* edited by Richard B. Morris.

These are only a few of the books and articles in store for you. And I mean literally in store. Your local library has them or your librarian can suggest many other books to read in your pursuit of the history of your country. I know, because in writing books I have had the greatest and wisest help from the libraries in and near my home town. But remember this: Never ask librarians anything you don't really want to know! They'll never stop until they find the answer.

So, happy reading in the days ahead. Don't get the idea that it was only Columbus who discovered America. That's a job for you as well!

INDEX

THE **GETTING TO KNOW** BOOKS

COVER TODAY'S WORLD

Africa

GETTING TO KNOW AFRICA'S FRENCH COMMUNITY
GETTING TO KNOW ALGERIA
GETTING TO KNOW THE CONGO RIVER
GETTING TO KNOW EGYPT
GETTING TO KNOW KENYA
GETTING TO KNOW LIBERIA
GETTING TO KNOW NIGERIA
GETTING TO KNOW THE SAHARA
GETTING TO KNOW SOUTH AFRICA
GETTING TO KNOW RHODESIA,
    ZAMBIA AND MALAWI
GETTING TO KNOW TANZANIA

Arctic

GETTING TO KNOW THE ARCTIC

Asia

GETTING TO KNOW BURMA
GETTING TO KNOW THE CENTRAL HIMALAYAS
GETTING TO KNOW HONG KONG
GETTING TO KNOW INDIA
GETTING TO KNOW JAPAN
GETTING TO KNOW THE NORTHERN HIMALAYAS
GETTING TO KNOW PAKISTAN
GETTING TO KNOW THE RIVER GANGES
GETTING TO KNOW THAILAND
GETTING TO KNOW THE TWO CHINAS
GETTING TO KNOW THE TWO KOREAS
GETTING TO KNOW THE TWO VIETNAMS

Caribbean and Central America

GETTING TO KNOW THE BRITISH WEST INDIES
GETTING TO KNOW COSTA RICA, EL SALVADOR
    AND NICARAGUA
GETTING TO KNOW CUBA
GETTING TO KNOW GUATEMALA
    AND THE TWO HONDURAS
GETTING TO KNOW MEXICO
GETTING TO KNOW PANAMA
GETTING TO KNOW PUERTO RICO
GETTING TO KNOW THE VIRGIN ISLANDS

Europe; East and West

GETTING TO KNOW EASTERN EUROPE
GETTING TO KNOW ENGLAND, SCOTLAND, IRELAND
    AND WALES
GETTING TO KNOW FRANCE
GETTING TO KNOW GREECE
GETTING TO KNOW ITALY

GETTING TO KNOW POLAND
GETTING TO KNOW SCANDINAVIA
GETTING TO KNOW SPAIN
GETTING TO KNOW SWITZERLAND
GETTING TO KNOW THE SOVIET UNION
GETTING TO KNOW THE TWO GERMANYS

Middle East

GETTING TO KNOW IRAN-IRAQ
GETTING TO KNOW ISRAEL
GETTING TO KNOW LEBANON
GETTING TO KNOW SAUDI ARABIA
GETTING TO KNOW THE TIGRIS
    AND EUPHRATES RIVERS
GETTING TO KNOW TURKEY

North America

GETTING TO KNOW ALASKA
GETTING TO KNOW AMERICAN INDIANS TODAY
GETTING TO KNOW CANADA
GETTING TO KNOW THE MISSISSIPPI RIVER
GETTING TO KNOW THE U.S.A.

Pacific

GETTING TO KNOW AUSTRALIA
GETTING TO KNOW HAWAII
GETTING TO KNOW INDONESIA
GETTING TO KNOW MALAYSIA AND SINGAPORE
GETTING TO KNOW THE PHILIPPINES
GETTING TO KNOW THE SOUTH PACIFIC

South America

GETTING TO KNOW ARGENTINA
GETTING TO KNOW BRAZIL
GETTING TO KNOW CHILE
GETTING TO KNOW COLOMBIA
GETTING TO KNOW PERU
GETTING TO KNOW THE RIVER AMAZON
GETTING TO KNOW VENEZUELA

United Nations Agencies

GETTING TO KNOW F.A.O.
GETTING TO KNOW
    THE HUMAN RIGHTS COMMISSION
GETTING TO KNOW UNESCO
GETTING TO KNOW UNICEF
GETTING TO KNOW THE UNITED NATIONS
    PEACE FORCES
GETTING TO KNOW W H O
GETTING TO KNOW WMO

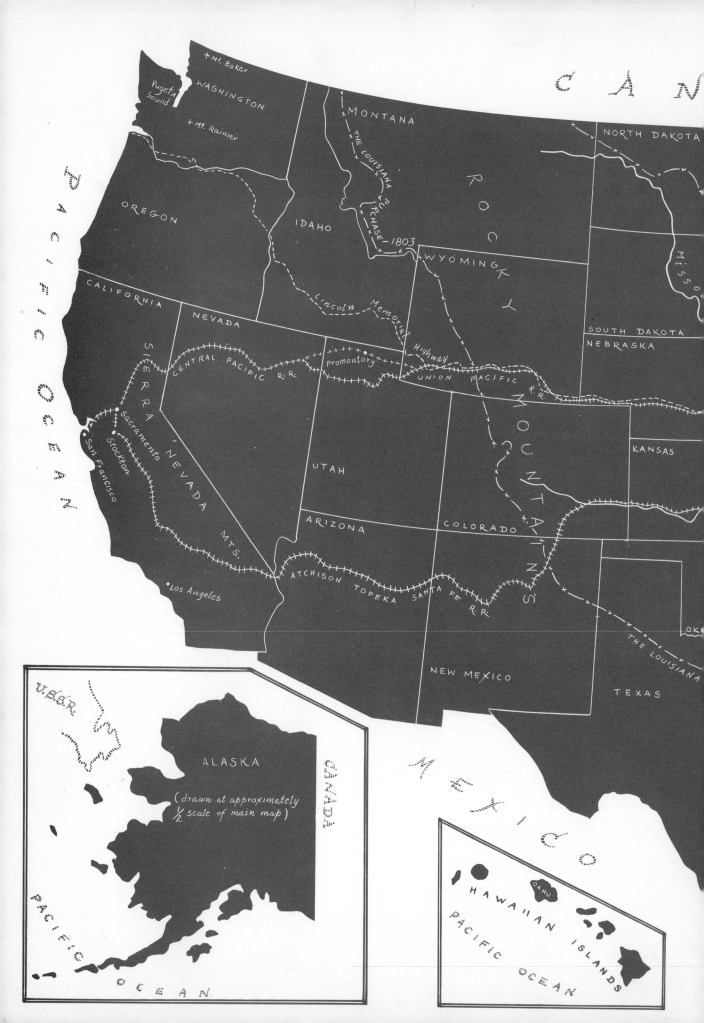